LEADING
WOMEN

Eva Perón

LESLI J. FAVOR

Marshall Cavendish
Benchmark
New York

Other Marshall Cavendish Offices:
Marshall Cavendish International (Asia) Private Limited, 1 New Industrial Road, Singapore 536196 • Marshall Cavendish International (Thailand) Co Ltd., 253 Asoke, 12th Flr., Sukhumvit 21 Road, Klongtoey Nua, Wattana, Bangkok 10110, Thailand • Marshall Cavendish (Malaysia) Sdn Bhd, Times Subang, Lot 46, Subang Hi-Tech Industrial Park, Batu Tiga, 40000 Shah Alam, Selangor Darul Ehsan, Malaysia

Marshall Cavendish is a trademark of Times Publishing Limited
All websites were available and accurate when this book was sent to press.

Library of Congress Cataloging-in-Publication Data
Favor, Lesli J.
Eva Perón / by Lesli J. Favor.
p. cm. — (Leading women)
Summary: "Presents the biography of Eva Perón against the backdrop of her political, historical, and cultural environment"—Provided by publisher. Includes bibliographical references and index.
ISBN 978-0-7614-4962-1
1. Perón, Eva, 1919-1952—Juvenile literature. 2. Argentina—History—1943-1955—Juvenile literature. 3. Women politicians—Argentina—Biography—Juvenile literature. 4. Presidents' spouses—Argentina—Biography—Juvenile literature. I. Title.
F2849.P37F38 2010
982.06'2092—dc22 [B]
2009029671

Editor: Deborah Grahame   Art Director: Anahid Hamparian
Publisher: Michelle Bisson   Series Designer: Nancy Sabato
Photo research by Connie Gardner

Cover photo by Daytona Beach News-Journal/AP Photo
The photographs in this book are used by permission and through the courtesy of: *Alamy*: Fabian von Poser, 1, 100; Pictorial Press, 42; *Museo Evita*: 19, 22; *Corbis*: Bettmann, 39, 50, 77, 80; *The Image Works*: Mary Evans Picture Library, 26; *Everett Collection*: 46, 97; *Getty Images*: Hulton Archive, 4, 6-7, 36, 44, 66, 70; Robert Harding World Imagery, 16; The Image Bank, 24; Time and Life Pictures, 29, 54, 58, 63; V. Stringer, 34, 85; AFP, 86, 90, 92; Popperfoto, 88.

Printed in Malaysia (T)
135642

CONTENTS

CHAPTER ONE

Day of Renunciation

O N A MIDSUMMER'S AFTERNOON IN 1951, a slim, blond woman swept her deep brown eyes over a crowd of more than a million people. They chanted her name: "Evita! Evita!" Everywhere she looked, she saw faces filled with hope, with longing, with anticipation. This was the most famous woman in Argentina. Indeed, on this afternoon of August 22, 1951, she may have been the most famous woman in the world.

Since dawn, people from across the country had been pouring into the *Avenida 9 de Julio*, a wide boulevard in Buenos Aires, the nation's capital. Workers had built a huge platform atop supports to form a stage. They had unfurled two billboard-size portraits of the guests of honor, President Juan Domingo Perón and his wife, Maria Eva Duarte de Perón. Between these 60-foot- (18-meter-) high portraits was a banner that read *"Perón-Eva Perón, la fórmula de la patria"* ("Perón-Eva Perón, the formula of the homeland").

This festive event was a political rally. On this day, the nation's largest trade union association, the *Confederación General del Trabajo* (General Confederation of Labor, or CGT), would formally support President Juan Perón for reelection. Of greater interest to the throngs of voters, however, was the question of Eva Perón's place on the ticket. Rumors swirled that today she would announce her candidacy as vice president. No woman in the world had held such a position. Would Eva Perón, a passionate supporter of the working class, be the first to achieve this rank?

Eva Perón makes a passionate speech during demonstrations by the General Confederation of Labor to persuade President Juan Perón to run for reelection.

At 5:00 PM there was movement on the stage. The crowd watched closely as President Perón walked onto the stage, along with governmental officials and CGT leaders. But where was Eva—Evita, as she was fondly known?

CGT president José Espejo began his speech. The crowd, however, would have none of it. They interrupted him again and again, calling, "Evita! Evita!" Suspense grew as Espejo announced that Eva Perón was not present tonight. He then left the stage. Soon, in a turn of events that clearly had been planned, he returned with Evita.

Eva Perón speaks to a crowd of more than a million people, who wait to learn whether she will declare her candidacy for the vice presidency.

In her dramatic, passionate style, Evita spoke to the crowd. As always, she painted herself as a loving servant of the poor. She assured them of her loyalty and affection, and she hinted at the animosity she felt for the oligarchy—the wealthy, powerful people who controlled the country. Speaking with her hands, she stretched her arms out toward the people in her familiar way.

The crowd had heard all these things from Evita before.

Tonight, they wanted to hear just one thing: that she would run for vice president. Again and again, they interrupted her with cries of *"Con Evita!"* ("With Evita!") and *"Evita con Perón!"* ("Evita with Perón!"). Evita, however, kept them in suspense. She ended her speech by saying,

> **I shall always do what the people wish, but I tell you, just as I said five years ago, that I would rather be Evita than the wife of the President, if this Evita could do anything for the pain of my country;**
>
> **and so now I say**
> **I would rather be Evita. . . .**

With this declaration, she gave the microphone to President Perón.

President Perón delivered his speech and formally accepted the nomination for president. But the crowd was not content to let the evening end like this. They interrupted the president repeatedly, calling for Evita's inclusion on the ticket.

Finally, the president's acceptance speech was over. Espejo returned to the microphone. To the delight of the crowd, he repeated their request: that Evita agree to run for the position of vice president. He carried the microphone to her.

By now it was dusk. People in the crowd had begun making torches with rolled-up newspapers. Evita swept her eyes over the million-plus people, lit by firelight. She pleaded with them not to force her to make a declaration tonight. At first, she begged for four days to think it over. Since the rally had been planned in advance, she had decided exactly what to do. Her rhetoric at this crucial moment was calculated, planned.

The workers in the crowd began to chant that they would go on strike (stop reporting to work) to win her agreement. To be heard over the uproar, Evita stated, "Comrades," four times. When she could be heard again, she said,

> **Comrades, I am not giving up my place in the struggle, I am only giving up the honors. I am keeping my hopes . . . for your glory and your love and that of General Perón.**

Again she asked for more time to decide, and again the crowd demanded a declaration tonight. She continued her speech.

> **Comrades, it's said throughout the world that I am a selfish and ambitious woman; you know very well that this isn't the case.**
> But you also know that everything I did, it was
> never so that I could have any political position
> in my country. I don't want any worker of my

> country to lack arguments when those people full of resentment, those mediocre people who never understand me and do not believe that everything I did, I did for the lowest motives. . . . **"**

Ironically, as Evita spoke these words, she stood beneath a huge poster of herself that suggested more political ambition than she was admitting to. The uproar about whether she would declare her candidacy was no surprise to her tonight. However, she said,

> **"** This has taken me by surprise. For a long time, I had known that my name was being put forward and I did not discourage it; I did it for the people and Perón . . . but never in my ordinary heart of an Argentine woman did I think I would be able to accept that post. . . . **"**

The crowd interrupted Evita again and again, until her speech became a sort of dialogue with them. As they urged her for a decision

GROUNDBREAKING WOMEN

In 1951, no woman had ever been elected to Argentina's executive branch of government. These positions—president, vice president, and cabinet ministers—had always been filled by men. In fact, Argentine women did not have the right to vote until 1947. The idea of a woman running for such a powerful public office was a groundbreaking concept at that time.

More than twenty more years would pass before a woman would become vice president. This woman was Isabel Martínez de Perón (1931–), who married Juan Perón in 1961. Isabel and Juan Perón were elected vice president and president in 1973. On July 1, 1974, Juan Perón died, and Isabel became president of Argentina. Less than a year later, the military took over the government and ended her term.

The first woman to be elected president of Argentina was Cristina Fernández de Kirchner (1953–). She took office in December 2007.

now, she kept reducing the amount of time she needed, from four days to one day to one night, and finally, to two hours. At this point she returned the microphone to Espejo.

Playing into the drama of the evening, Espejo announced, "We shall wait here for her decision. We shall not move until she gives us a reply in accordance with the desires of the people." And everyone settled in to wait.

After the highly charged evening of speeches and chants, the rally ended rather abruptly. Evita finally returned to the microphone. But rather than announce her decision, she said only, "Comrades, as General Perón has said, I will do what the people say." With this enigmatic statement, the rally was over. People drifted away. They still wondered whether Eva Perón had agreed to run for vice president or not.

BEHIND THE SCENES

Behind the scenes, a number of forces were at work to prevent Evita's name from making it onto the ballot. The main obstacle was that no woman had held such a high-ranking position of power in the government. If the president were to die in office, the vice president would step in as president. A woman president would be new—and, to some people, scary. Another obstacle was the military, a powerful force in Argentina. Military leaders were not ready to accept Evita as second in line in power—and their potential boss.

Finally, President Perón himself was an obstacle. To the public, he appeared to accept Evita's bid for office. After all, there were the banners and posters with their two images together, and he had not stopped them from being handed out. But privately, he did not give Evita his support to run for vice president. Evita was confused.

According to biographer Alicia Dujovne Ortiz, Evita said, "Perón has abandoned me. I've asked him what to do one thousand times, and one thousand times he answered, 'Your conscience will tell you what to do.'"

THE RENUNCIATION

Nine days after the political rally, Evita gave an emotional radio address. In it, she stated her decision to renounce (take back) the honor of running for vice president. Her only ambition, she said, was

> **"that it should be said of me . . . that there was by the side of Perón a woman who devoted her life to the task of conveying to the President the people's hopes and that the people lovingly used to call this woman 'Evita.'**
>
> **That is all I wish to be."**

After that, the day of the rally—August 22, 1951—became known as Evita's "day of renunciation."

What was so important about this woman, Eva Perón, that her decision about political office would transfix the nation in this way? For it was not just Evita's supporters who were riveted by the election drama. Her detractors were, too. While much of the nation loved Evita, another big part of the populace hated her.

Evita had done what no other Argentine woman had ever done. She had risen from poverty, unimportance, and illegitimacy to become the most powerful woman in the nation. She had grown up poor, but now she wore designer gowns, furs, and lavish jewelry. She had gone from being a village girl to being an actress and then a vice president's wife—all before her thirtieth birthday. All these hard-won accomplishments inspired the admiration of the working class. To them, she was a hero, an example of what they themselves could aspire to. But to Argentina's wealthy citizens, she was an impostor who had weaseled her way in where she didn't belong.

Behind the drama of the campaigns and speeches, Evita was waging a personal battle. She had cancer. At the time of the political rally, she probably did not know how serious her condition was. In fact, she probably was unaware that she had cancer, since she had refused to consult a doctor. But she could not hold off the disease with denials. By the time she consulted doctors, it was too late. Within a year, she had died.

With Evita's death, millions of Argentines fell into deep mourning and shock. To many, it seemed appropriate when an organization of workers suggested she be made a saint. Others privately celebrated her death, however. They saw her only as a power-hungry, poor girl who had used her beauty and greed to climb her way to the top.

A few years later, it would become illegal to have photographs of Evita. Such was the hatred and fear of Peronism, the political belief system of Juan and Evita Perón. What could account for two such opposite views of the same person? The answers lie in Evita's closely guarded personal history, something few people in the nation knew anything about.

CHAPTER TWO

Pursuit of a Dream

E VITA HAD NOT ALWAYS LED A LIFE OF power, privilege, and prosperity. Her life began humbly, on the wide, flat plains of central Argentina. This region was blanketed with cattle ranches and farms. Railroads snaked across the landscape. Towns here were small. Most of them were villages that sprang up around train stops. In one of these villages, Los Toldos, Eva María Duarte was born on May 7, 1919.

Evita was the youngest of five children born to Juan Duarte and Juana Ibarguren. Evita was the fourth girl, after Elisa, Blanca, and Erminda. Juan, the middle child, was their brother. In those days, men often worked far from home. It was common for a man to have a "first family" with his wife in his hometown, as well as a "second family" with a mistress, perhaps near where he worked. Juana Ibarguren and her five children were Juan Duarte's second family. The children took the Duarte name, but their parents were never married.

At the time of Evita's birth, Juan was the successful manager of a large farm near Los Toldos. He did not own the farm—it belonged to wealthy landowners—but he did own a small amount of land that his employers had given him. He also had a car and a house on the main street in Los Toldos. He gained even more status when he was appointed justice of the peace, a type of judge. Well liked and socially active, Juan Duarte provided a comfortable home for his second family. Townspeople knew that Juan and Juana were not married, but they overlooked it.

Argentine cowboys ride in the pampas. Eva Duarte grew up in small towns in this vast, flat, grassy region of Argentina.

THE PAMPA

The landscape of Evita's childhood was the *pampa*, a vast, mainly flat grassland. This plain stretches from the Andes Mountains in the west to the city of Buenos Aires on the east coast. Evita's childhood town of Los Toldos was in the wetter eastern portion. Here, some trees grew among tall grasses, and fields of wheat helped feed the nation.

To the west, the pampa is drier. Out there, millions of cattle graze the grasslands, and *gauchos*, or cowboys, watch over the herds. When Evita was young, Argentina was already known worldwide for its beef production. Though poor, Evita's family would have eaten plenty of beef.

CHILDHOOD WITHOUT A FATHER

Before Evita was a year old, however, Juan Duarte cut ties with his second family and returned to Chivilcoy, about 20 miles (32 kilometers) away. Baby Evita's quality of life took a turn for the worse. The family's social standing and small luxuries disappeared with her father. Historians still do not know why Juan left. But the fact remains that Evita grew up fatherless.

Eva Duarte's father, Juan Duarte.

Left with no money, Juana Ibarguren moved her "small tribe," as she liked to call her children, to a tiny house near the railroad tracks. The kitchen was a shed in the back. Evita learned to walk and talk in this cramped house, as the sound of passing trains filled the air. She also learned that townspeople could be cruel and judgmental. Without Juan there to smooth the way, people rejected and avoided Evita and her siblings. They were the children of unmarried parents.

To earn a living, Juana Ibarguren sewed townspeople's clothes. From early morning to late at night, she sat at her foot-powered machine. Even with varicose (swollen) veins in her legs, she kept at her work and refused to rest. The sound of her sewing machine blended with the sound of passing trains, becoming the haunting music of Evita's childhood.

In January 1926, when Evita was six years old, Juan Duarte died in a car accident. Social custom would have kept Juana Ibarguren away from the funeral, but she had a stubborn streak. She packed up her five children and made the 20-mile (32-km) journey to Chivilcoy. After an argument at the door, Juan's "second family" was allowed inside for the wake. From there, they walked to the cemetery, where the funeral was held.

Evita was too young to have any memory of her father at the time of his death. As an adult, she never talked about this time in her life, or of her childhood in general.

SCHOOL

Evita did not start school until she was eight years old. Wearing a white smock, or long jacket, like the other girls, she started the first grade. The elementary school had only one teacher, but the children studied such diverse subjects as chemistry and zoology. Evita was often absent from school, but she performed fairly well—neither at the top nor at the bottom of her class. Her teacher later remembered her only as a quiet, large-eyed child. Evita attended this school for two years.

Meanwhile, Evita's eldest sister, Elisa, had gotten a job at the post office in Los Toldos. Her income was a welcome addition to Juana Ibarguren's earnings. But life grew complicated. Elisa had gotten her job through the influence of Juan Duarte's friends, members of the Conservative Party. Around the time Evita started school, however, the Radical Party came to power. The new mayor of Los Toldos, a radical, fired Elisa. At Juana Ibarguren's request, however, he found her a new job at the post office in Junín, about 20 miles (32 km) away.

JUNÍN

And so, in early 1930, when Evita was ten years old, she moved to Junín with her family. This town was located between the vast pampa and the nation's capital, Buenos Aires. The railway passed through Junín and the neighborhoods surrounding the town. Evita's family did not live in a shack by the tracks in this town, however. The three older siblings had jobs now, so the family could afford to live in a small villa, or house. Juana Ibarguren was finally able to quit sewing. She made a little money by cooking meals for single men who lived nearby.

Evita's new school was near the town's main square. Even here, rumors about her family followed her. She had few friends. Parents would not allow their children to play with Evita. One of Evita's teachers described her as a "very beautiful little girl with dark hair and skin like porcelain . . . a self-absorbed child with an intense inner life, great sensitivity and great vulnerability." Pictures of Evita at this age show a serious, unsmiling face with large dark eyes framed by short, dark hair.

It is no surprise that Evita daydreamed about a different life filled with glamour, riches, and adoration. By the time she was fifteen, one of her chief delights was clipping photographs of movie stars out of *Sintonía*. This popular film magazine was filled with articles and photographs of stars from Argentina and other countries. Evita and her sister clipped out photographs and exchanged them like trading cards. Evita would do Erminda's chore of washing dishes in exchange for more clippings.

Eva Duarte's mother, Juana Ibarguren.

Evita was especially drawn to Norma Shearer, an American actress. Shearer had risen from poverty to stardom in motion pictures. Evita's "intense inner life," noted by her teacher, included daydreams of her own rise from poverty to stardom.

Evita also liked to recite poetry. She was drawn to poems that dripped with emotion, and she would throw all of her energy into performing the words. One day, she stood outside the record store in town and recited poems through a loudspeaker that the store had set up. Years later, Evita's sister Blanca recalled, "For the first time Evita's voice was broadcast over the airwaves. She recited a wide repertoire of poems with the same conviction and professionalism which would later help her to conquer the Capital as an actress."

Evita became interested in acting, and she performed in a production at school. At home, she practiced her recital and acting skills. Again and again, she told her mother that she would become an actress one day. Juana Ibarguren refused to accept Evita's declarations. One of the men who often dined with the family, José Alvarez Rodriguez, cautioned Juana not to limit Evita's dreams. If Evita had talent, she should be allowed to follow her dreams. If she did not have talent, then Juana should encourage Evita anyway. Still, Evita's dreams continued to cause tension between Evita and her mother.

Evita's mother did not realize how soon Evita's dreams would lead her away—and how high she would soar in success.

LEAVING HOME

The exact details of when and how Evita left Junín for Buenos Aires are unknown. Various stories swirl around this important transition. According to one popular account, the fifteen-year-old fell madly in love with a tango singer, Agustín Magaldi, who performed in Junín. She begged the singer to take her to Buenos Aires. It is true that Magaldi's voice was magnificent—he was one of the most popular tango singers of the day. His record *Vagabundo* had sold over a million copies. But as biographers Nicholas Fraser and Marysa Navarro

TANGO

Argentine tango was born in the late 1800s in the neighborhoods around Buenos Aires. Tango is a type of music and dance known for its passion and drama. It is also very sensual, since the pair of dancers often embrace as they "walk" to the music. Their regal carriage, rhythmic movements, and showy poses help the audience "see" the music.

Because of the physical contact between dancers, tango was at first popular only in the lower classes. Polite society frowned on this sort of public touching. But after the dance spread to Uruguay, Europe, and beyond, Argentina's wealthy people finally accepted tango.

point out, "There is no record of the tango singer's having come to Junín that year."

More believable is the story that Juana Ibarguren reluctantly took Evita to Buenos Aires. More than sixty years later, in 1997, Evita's sister Blanca wrote, "I can still remember Mother's irritation and the climate of nervousness and sadness that prevailed in our house on the day our mother accompanied Evita to Buenos Aires. Evita, however, was confident and serene." Blanca tells how, by the end of the day, Evita had been offered a "small contract" as a radio performer. From that day on, Evita lived in Buenos Aires. Evita's dream, it seemed, was within reach.

CHAPTER THREE

Rise to Stardom

W HEN EVITA ARRIVED IN BUENOS AIRES, she set aside her childhood. Gone were the quiet, predictable days of village life in Junín. In their place, fifteen-year-old Evita discovered the exciting and changeable days of her nation's capital. In 1936, the year after Evita arrived, Buenos Aires had 2.5 million residents. It was the third-largest city in the world, after New York City and Chicago. Evita never said whether the enormous city seemed overwhelming, or whether she felt lost in the sea of strangers. But actions showed her determination to make a place for herself in this vast city.

BUENOS AIRES

Buenos Aires sprang up on the Río de la Plata, an estuary that separates Argentina from Uruguay on the east coast of South America. (An estuary is an arm of the sea that reaches inward to meet one or more rivers, in this case the Uruguay and Paraná rivers.) Natives of Buenos Aires called themselves *porteños*, meaning "people of the port." Their ancestors had arrived in this port city by boat from Italy, Germany, Spain, Ireland, England, Greece, Poland, and other distant places. In contrast, Argentines from the rest of the country were called *campesinos*, meaning "people from the countryside." Evita, a native of the pampa, was a campesina.

A bird's-eye view of the *Avenida 9 de Julio* in Buenos Aires in 1947. At 426 feet (130 meters) wide, the boulevard is the widest in the world. The Obelisk in the center is a monument to the founding of the city in 1536.

Buenos Aires was a diverse city at the heart of the nation. Here, Argentina's president and other government officials had offices in the Casa Rosada, a large, pink building at the east end of the Plaza de Mayo. The Buenos Aires Stock Exchange and the leading banks were in Buenos Aires. So, too, were the growing industries of publishing, radio, and film. For someone in the United States, the city of Buenos Aires would be like having Washington, D.C. New York City, and Hollywood rolled into one place. The railroad that had run near Evita's house in Los Toldos led to Buenos Aires. The other railways lacing the country also led there, bringing not just campesinos but also cattle to be slaughtered and exported.

THE OLIGARCHY

Buenos Aires was home to many of the nation's wealthiest and most powerful people. They led luxurious lifestyles filled with shopping and socializing. They attended cultural events such as the opera at the Colón Theater. They followed European fashions, and their houses were inspired by European architecture. They had household servants and private tutors, and they hired people like Evita's father, Juan Duarte, to manage their farms and ranches in the pampa. In fact, a small number of wealthy Argentines owned most of the land in the country. During the summer, they gathered their bags and their servants and went to Europe. Some chose to live in Europe permanently.

This elite class of people was very powerful. They behaved as though Argentina were theirs alone. In fact, they were a lot like royalty. Even though the middle and lower classes far outnumbered the upper class, the masses had little influence in the government;

In 1939, wealthy Argentines attend a society party.

they had little say over their rights and opportunities. With a bitter tone, they referred to the upper class as the *oligarchy*, a term
used to refer to a class of people that holds governmental power
over all classes.

At age fifteen, Evita had already experienced the oligarchy's influence. She had grown up among the poor, a class of citizens who had

little representation in government. All the respect her family had once enjoyed was gone after Juan Duarte had left Los Toldos.

BECOMING AN ACTOR

When Evita arrived in Buenos Aires, she showed no interest in politics. She would have seen little opportunity for women to serve in government, anyway. Argentine women did not have the right to vote at that time, and they did not hold powerful government positions. Actors, however, seemed to lead glamorous lives filled with some of the same luxuries that the oligarchy enjoyed. This lifestyle appealed to Evita.

But a luxurious lifestyle was still just a dream to Evita. She rented a tiny room in a drab, cheap boardinghouse and survived on little money and little food. Soon the small radio contract ended, and she was unemployed. She made the rounds of the theaters in the city and auditioned for parts. Evita got several small roles with the Argentine Comedy Company. One of the first reviews of her acting stated that she was "very precise in her brief appearances."

A year later, Evita was hired by a touring theatrical company. They traveled around Argentina and put on plays, such as *What . . . Me Work? Never*. Evita's roles were small, and she received little pay. With these wages she had to pay not only for her food and lodging, but also for her costumes for the performances. She sent what little money she could save to her mother in Junín.

Actors in these small parts received little respect or appreciation from either their employers or the public. It was understood that no "respectable" girl went into acting, and well-to-do people looked down on the profession. These judgmental attitudes were not much

RADIO BROADCASTING

Even before she went into politics, Evita earned at least a footnote in history. She played a small part in building Argentina's young radio industry.

Radio broadcasting as it is known today was developed in the 1920s. Before then, broadcasts consisted mainly of Morse code. Their purpose was usually to communicate important messages, not to entertain people. Then, in the early 1920s, radio operators began to broadcast live performances such as operas. By 1924, five radio stations existed in Buenos Aires.

When Evita began working in radio in the late 1930s, the largest Argentine station was Radio El Mundo. Its stylish headquarters had seven studios where broadcasts were performed.

The radio company that Evita and Pascual Pelliciotta formed in 1939 was much smaller than Radio El Mundo. Evita's brother, Juan, gave Evita's career a boost by arranging for Guerreno, a maker of bath soap, to sponsor Evita's programs for the next five years. As sponsor, Guerreno paid to air commercials during the show, thereby providing the company's income. The arrangement was successful. Within a year, the little company merged with Radio Argentina, which soon after merged with Radio El Mundo. Evita's small company had become a building block in the most important radio station in the country.

different from the criticism Evita had suffered as an illegitimate child in the pampa villages.

The touring company returned to Buenos Aires and closed down. Evita again sought work. Over the next two years, she sometimes found employment in theater. Her roles were always small, and some of them were nonspeaking parts. In December 1936 she had a tiny part—lasting just a few minutes—in *The Children's Hour*. Many years later, another actor in that play described Evita to biographers Nicholas Fraser and Marysa Navarro:

" [She was] young and pretty, very pretty; with dark eyes, deep red lips and a skin the color and texture of a magnolia, quite transparent. She seemed a personification of innocence and that is really what she was, very pure inside. . . . "

Barely scraping together a living, Evita found other small jobs. She got another small radio contract, hosted a dance contest, and was an extra in a movie. None of the jobs paid well, but during these years, Evita was learning the system. She observed how actors made contacts in the business and how they created a public image. She improved her acting skills with help from a mentor, Pierina Desalessi.

During the 1930s radio broadcasting became a thriving industry in Argentina. By the end of the decade, the country had the second-largest radio network in the world, next to that of the United States. The stations broadcast music, news, sports, and soap operas. Aired in half-hour "chapters," the soaps were enormously popular. Just as people today tune in faithfully to their favorite television programs, people in the 1930s tuned in to favorite radio soaps. While they listened to the actors' dialogue and the sound effects, they created mental pictures of the characters and events. This method of storytelling included listeners in the creative process.

SUCCESS

Some time after 1937 Evita's career reached a tipping point and began to take off. She turned her attention from stage acting to radio performing. In 1939 she and a partner, Pascual Pelliciotta, formed their own radio company and started producing soaps. By now, Evita had regular work as a soap actress. By the end of the decade the actress, scarcely twenty years old, saw her name appear frequently in newspaper gossip columns. She saw her face gracing the pages of magazines. *Sintonía* featured a glamorous photograph of her on the cover.

By 1943 Evita was living in an apartment in a fine neighborhood and enjoyed a sizable income. It seemed that all of her dreams and hard work were paying off. She told an interviewer,

Eva Duarte was a radio performer and screen actress in Buenos Aires in the late 1930s and 1940s.

> **Here I have reached the height of my career, a very rewarding career which began modestly but grew as I dedicated myself to my work, as I strove to perfect myself and to assimilate [take in] the very valuable lessons I received.**

The star, just now reaching her mid-twenties, believed that she had reached the height of her career. No one—least of all Evita—suspected that her career would soon change course and make her a worldwide legend.

CHAPTER FOUR

A "Marvelous Day"

E VITA DUARTE MET COLONEL Juan Domingo Perón, her future husband and the future president of Argentina, by chance. Later, Evita referred to the day they met as her "marvelous day." In that first meeting, both Evita and Juan felt the attraction.

It all began with an earthquake. On the evening of January 15, 1944, the town of San Juan, near the border with Chile, was struck by intense shaking. Buildings fell into rubble, and thousands of people were crushed and killed. The town was destroyed. In the final tally, an estimated ten thousand people lost their lives. The earthquake is remembered as one of the worst natural disasters in the country's history.

More than 621 miles (1,000 km) away, tremors from the earthquake reached Buenos Aires. When details of the disaster finally began to pour into the nation's capital, people were shocked by the degree of destruction. President Ramírez went to examine the damage in San Juan. Back in Buenos Aires, Colonel Juan Domingo Perón, Argentina's secretary of labor, took charge of raising money to help victims of the disaster.

One of Colonel Perón's ideas was to involve glamorous entertainers in the fundraising. He wanted performers from radio, film, and theater to walk through the streets of Buenos Aires, along with military personnel in dress (formal) uniforms. They would carry donation boxes to offer to citizens watching the parade. Perón also planned a lavish party to be held at a

Eva Duarte in 1944, the year she met Juan Perón.

JUAN PERÓN (1895-1974)

Juan Domingo Perón was one of the most influential Argentines of the twentieth century. Like Evita, he was born to a lower-class family in the pampa. He, too, remained loyal to his working-class roots even after he rose to power.

Juan's father, Mario Tomás Perón, was a tenant farmer, and his mother, Juana Toledo, was a household servant. In 1899, the family moved to a sheep ranch in Patagonia. This is the cold, dry southern region of Argentina. Here, Juan developed a love of the outdoors and became an accomplished horseback rider. Starting at the age of nine, he spent school years staying with relatives in Buenos Aires and returned home to Patagonia for the summers. At age fifteen, he entered the National Military College.

Military life suited Juan, and he rose steadily in the ranks. In 1924 he was promoted to captain, and the next year he began three years of advanced military studies. During this time he married his first wife, Aurelia Tizón. She later died of cancer—the same disease that eventually killed Evita. From 1930 to 1936, Juan was a professor of military history. He also served as a private secretary to the minister of war.

By the time Juan met Evita in early 1944, he was a colonel. Colonel Perón was an attractive, muscular man with a wide, bright smile. His was a gifted public speaker, and he already had developed loyal friends and supporters. He was ready for greatness, as soon as the right opportunity presented itself.

As a teenager, Juan Perón began training for a future in the military.

stadium. Tickets to the event would bring in more funds for the earthquake victims.

Colonel Perón asked the actors to come to his offices at the Secretariat of Labor to get the donation boxes. Here, in the bustle of actors, he first met Evita. She was, he recalled later, "a mass of nerves," yet eager to help the people of San Juan. She suggested that he keep things simple and have the actors walk through the better parts of town, as people there would be most able to give.

At the end of the week, Evita and a friend attended the expensive party at Luna Park stadium. She wore tasteful 1940s fashion: a black dress, long gloves, and a white hat. During the course of the evening, she made her way over to Colonel Perón—as did many other guests—to pay her respects to the host. Apparently, the evening solidified the attraction between the actor and the colonel. After that night they began dating, and before long Evita had moved into the colonel's apartment.

RISING STARS

Meanwhile, Juan Perón's career was on the rise. When he and Evita met in January, he was the secretary of labor, and he also worked in the ministry of war. He was a founding member of an influential military group called the *Grupo de Oficiales Unidos* (United Group of Officers), or GOU. With these positions and connections, Perón had become a powerful figure in government. When Perón's boss at the ministry of war became Argentina's president in February 1944, Perón was promoted to minister of war.

The pairing of Evita Duarte and Colonel Juan Perón had ripple effects on both their careers. Soon after the fundraising party, the couple posed for a photograph, along with a friend of Perón's and the director of the radio station where Evita worked. The photograph was published in a movie magazine. In effect, it introduced the new power couple to the nation. It was the first of many photographs of Evita and Juan that found their way into the media.

Before she met Perón, Evita had created a radio program called *Heroines of History*. Each episode, scripted by Francisco José Muñoz Azpiri, was to be about a different famous woman from history. The series was tailor made for Evita, who would play the part of each famous woman. After meeting Juan Perón, Evita went back to work on the series. Given the high-profile nature of her new relationship, the radio station began to advertise the series more heavily. Evita also received a large raise in pay—the "biggest contract to date in radio broadcasting," Evita told an interviewer.

Soon after this, Evita created the glamorous image that would become her trademark—the look she was known for. She bleached her brown hair blond. This change showed off her pale, clear skin and large, dark eyes. It is this look that people remember best.

Evita originally changed her hair color for a film role. Arriving on set, she behaved with an exaggerated air of confidence and referred repeatedly to her relationship with Perón. She spoke highly of the colonel and encouraged everyone there to support him. She was taking the first step toward a mission that would later take over her life: speaking publicly to win political support for Perón. On the movie set, though, Evita's showy confidence caused conflict between her and the other star, Libertad Lamarque. One version of events describes the two women getting into a heated argument in which Libertad slapped Evita on the face.

The supposed slapping incident is significant because it marked a turning point, when two different images of Evita had taken shape. One image was that of a humble country girl who had risen to the top

LA EMINENTE PRIMERA ACTRIZ
CON SU SELECTO CONJUNTO EN
TRES MAGNIFICOS PROGRAMAS

A LAS 10.30 HORAS
odos los MIERCOLES y VIERNES

'HACIA UN
'UTURO MEJOR''

na audición de fino relieve espi-
tual, inspirada en elevados sen-
mientos argentinistas. Libretos de
RICARDO VIDELA.

A LAS 18 HORAS
Diariamente, de LUNES a VIERNES

''UN AMOR
EN LA INDIA''

Original de SALVADOR VALVER-
DE Una intensa radionovela cuya
acci   scurre en el exótico es-
cen   u India legendaria.

A LAS 22.30 HO
Diariamente, de LUNES a VI

''UNA MUJER
LAS BARRICAD

Original de RICARDO VI
Magnífica novela inspirada
heroica existencia de la famo
dame Chang Kai-Shek

This poster from the 1940s features a glamorous image of Evita Duarte above
the names and show times of three radio programs she performed.

of her career through hard work. The other image was that of a greedy, scheming girl who had done all she could to gain wealth and power. Through the rest of Evita's life and after her death, each image gained strength among the people. Today, these opposing views of Evita are known as the White Myth (favored by her supporters) and the Black Myth (favored by her enemies). Neither version is completely true—or completely false.

Early that same year, 1944, Evita played the lead role in a movie called *The Prodigal*. Only twenty-four years old, Evita was much younger than the character she played onscreen. However, Evita felt drawn to the selfless values of this character, who used her wealth to improve the lives of villagers near her large property. The woman is called "the mother of the poor" and "the sister of the sad"—nicknames of the sort that Argentina's poor would later invent for Evita. The tragic ending of the story also appealed to Evita. The woman's lover leaves her, she loses her land, and she kills herself.

Less than five months after Evita met Juan Perón, the broadcasting industry announced that the performers had formed a union. As part of a union, the performers could bargain with employers for better pay and other benefits. It was also announced that Evita Duarte would be the union's president. Juan Perón's influence most likely played a key role in this turn of events. The office of the secretary of labor formally recognized Evita's new position.

In mid-1944, Evita created another radio program. It was called *Toward a Better Future*. She used the program to broadcast propaganda supporting Perón. Each episode featured a commentator who would introduce a political topic and then introduce "The Woman." This woman, always played by Evita, would talk about politics in a normal, everyday voice. She always brought up the subject of Colonel Perón.

After rising to success as a radio performer, Eva Duarte led a glamorous lifestyle.

The program made it seem as though Perón was responsible for a great deal that had happened politically lately, whether this was true or not. The show's purpose was to build support for Perón among citizens who did not normally follow politics—citizens who lived like Evita Duarte once had. These people, the working class, far outnumbered the oligarchy. With their support, Perón might achieve his political goals.

In July 1944, during growing disorder within the government, Perón took office as vice president. Already he had become a political figure who attracted both firm support and firm opposition. As his power grew, people responded to him more and more strongly. They either supported Perón completely or opposed him strongly. Evita's presence in Perón's life attracted additional criticism from his opponents. Many people thought it was inappropriate for Perón to live with Evita unmarried and to allow her presence in some political meetings. It didn't help matters that Evita was an actor, and that she refused to reveal any personal information about herself. People wondered who Eva Duarte really was and how she fit in with Perón's political plans.

CHAPTER FIVE

Day of Revolution

EVEN BEFORE HE BECAME VICE PRESIDENT, Juan Perón had begun to shape the country. He made some of his first big changes when he was secretary of labor and social welfare. His job was to protect the rights of workers and support other types of social welfare, or public services. Perón believed workers should have the right to organize, to strike (to stop work in order to force an employer to do something), and to earn a guaranteed minimum wage. He also believed that workers should be able to earn pensions, which is money paid to workers after they retire from a job. He proposed legislation dealing with these and other social welfare issues. The legislation was signed into law.

Workers throughout the country benefited from Juan's work in the labor secretariat. For a long time, the government had mostly protected the interests of the oligarchy. Now, to the amazement of the working class, someone was looking out for them. They began to view Perón as their champion, and they gave him their loyalty. This loyalty would carry Perón into higher government offices.

Wealthy landowners and factory owners disliked the changes in labor laws. They became bitter toward Perón, who was responsible for the changes. Just as Perón earned loyalty from the working class, he earned a growing anger from the nation's wealthy citizens. In addition, some members of the army and

Eva Perón, shown speaking to a laborer in the 1940s, never lost her compassion for Argentina's working poor.

ARGENTINA AND WORLD WAR II

World War II (1939–1945) was the largest war that the world had ever known. An estimated 50 million people died worldwide. On one side were the Axis powers: Germany, Italy, and Japan. On the other side were the Allies, which included the Big Three powers: the British Empire, the Union of Soviet Socialist Republics (USSR), and the United States of America.

Although the war is called a "world" war, not every country participated. Argentina was one of the neutral countries. During the early 1940s, Argentina's government was a bit unstable. In 1943, the country's military overthrew its government and kicked out the conservative president. It was in the new, military-controlled government that Juan Perón rose to power.

During these years, the Allies watched Argentina closely. Was the government fascist, like Italy's? Would Argentina join forces with the Axis powers? At the end of the war, Argentina declared war on the Axis powers. The declaration happened in March 1945, only two months before the war ended in May.

The declaration, however late, caused political arguments within Argentina. Some people wanted to stay neutral and not support either side in the war. Others wanted to join the war to fight fascism and Nazism. In July, the government announced that elections would be held that year. Rather than calming citizens with hope for change, the announcement caused even more arguing. During this confusion and trouble, the Revolution of October 17, 1945, occurred.

some government officials opposed Juan's political agenda. They disliked and distrusted Perón. As Perón's power grew, these people became more outspoken about their unhappiness.

Evita was never far from Perón's side. She watched and listened as he did business and made speeches. During this time, her radio broadcasts spread a great deal of positive propaganda about Perón. Some of what she broadcast was true. However, members of the army did not like the fact that she presented Perón as the only military hero. Perón took Evita with him to many political functions. Some military officials feared that Evita had too much influence over Perón. They weren't sure who she really was or where she had come from, and Evita refused to answer questions about her past. This led to widespread rumors and gossip.

AN UNPOPULAR GOVERNMENT

As 1945 wore on, the military government became increasingly unpopular. Many different political groups in the country wanted a change. They focused their outrage on Juan Perón, and they claimed that the government had become fascist. This accusation was especially harsh, coming so soon after the Allied defeat of Nazi Germany and fascist Italy. (See the sidebar, Argentina and World War II, at left.)

Perón fought back against the attacks from political groups. His goal was to show the huge working class that he was on their side. He used nationalism, or strong devotion to one's country, to help his cause. He claimed that foreign powers were leading his opposition. Huge crowds of workers gathered to hear Perón speak and to cheer him on.

By October the political conflict surrounding Perón had reached a breaking point. On October 8, a group of army officers asked Perón to quit his job. He refused to do so. The next day, the officers met

On September 19, 1945, half a million people marched to protest Juan Perón and the military-run government.

EVA PERÓN

with the president. They promised a military coup d'etat, or takeover of the government, if Perón did not quit. This time, at the president's request, Perón left both the government and the military. On the same day, Evita was fired from her job at the radio station. It seemed that the two of them had suddenly hit bottom. They began to discuss the idea of retiring from public life and living happily together.

But the trouble was not over. Two days later, in Juan and Evita's apartment, Perón was arrested. He was held by the navy and hidden away on an island off the coast of Buenos Aires. This information, however, was kept secret from the public and even from Evita. They did not know whether Perón was alive or whether he would ever return.

The next week was terrible for Evita. Her only wish was to find out what had happened to Perón and to bring him back. Later she wrote about how she felt during these days:

"

. . . those eight days still hurt me—

and more, far more, than if I had

been able to spend them in his

company, sharing his anguish. . . .

I rushed into the streets looking for

friends who might still be able to do

▶

something for him. . . . I wandered about all the districts of the great city. Ever since then I have known all the kinds of hearts that beat under my country's sky. . . . Since that day I think it cannot be very difficult to die for a cause that one loves. Or, simply, to die for love. 𝄢

Evita tried to get a labor lawyer to help her get Perón released. Even though she went three times to ask for help, the lawyer refused. Then, on October 14, Evita received a letter from Perón. It was delivered by an army doctor who had visited Perón on the island. At last, she knew for certain that Perón was alive. In the letter, Perón called her "My adored treasure." He told her where he was and said he had written a letter to the president to ask for his release. He wrote,

> **" As soon as I get out we'll get married and go somewhere and live peacefully. "**

The doctor made copies of Juan's letter to the president, and he gave the copies to newspapers. Workers throughout the country raised their voices in Perón's support. They had good reason to be concerned. Perón was their champion. Without him, they might lose the rights and freedoms they had gained while he was in power. When the president claimed that Perón had not been arrested, the workers did not believe him. Strikes began breaking out in Buenos Aires and elsewhere.

OCTOBER 17, 1945

Trade union leaders organized a twenty-four-hour strike for October 18, but the course of events had gotten out of their control. On October 17, the day before the planned strike, workers across Buenos Aires gathered in the streets and marched to the Plaza de Mayo. Workers poured in from the countryside and streamed across the city. As the day continued, thousands upon thousands made their way to the Casa Rosada in search of news of Perón. They shouted for him. As darkness fell, they made torches from rolled newspapers.

Acting together like this, the workers were a powerful force. They had shut down the nation's capital city. Shops, companies, and even the government offices were unable to do business.

In February 1946, the newly married Juan and Eva Perón attended
a party thrown for Juan, who was running for president.

Deep emotion swept the crowd when, just after 11:00 PM, spotlights shone on the front of the Casa Rosada, and Juan Perón stepped out onto a balcony. Like a winning team, the crowd began cheering and celebrating. Thousands of voices chanted "Perón!" again and again. They wanted to know what had happened and where he had been.

Perón did not answer the questions, except to say that he wanted to leave all that had happened behind him. He said that he had retired from the army, and now he wanted to "mix with this sweating mass as a simple citizen." Finally, Perón told the crowd to go home and to take the next day off from work to celebrate. For many years thereafter, October 17 was celebrated as a national holiday called the Day of Revolution.

MARRIAGE

Where was Evita in all of this? Later, some people tried to claim that she had organized the entire workers' revolution on October 17. In reality, she did not yet have that kind of influence over the unions. That day Evita had stayed at home to keep out of danger, as Perón had asked her to.

Just as Perón's future was set on course that night, so was Evita's. The two did not retire quietly together. Instead, they joined forces, both personally and politically. Four days after Perón's release, they got married in a small civil ceremony. Five weeks later they held a religious marriage ceremony in a Catholic church. Then Perón announced that he would run for president of Argentina in the upcoming election, scheduled for February 24, 1946.

THE CAMPAIGN TRAIL

Evita never did return to acting. Instead, she turned the full force of her attention to Perón's presidential campaign. She traveled with him from town to town and stood beside him as he spoke to crowds. In each town, Perón promised to fight for the working class and to lessen the powers of the oligarchy. Evita made no speeches, but her presence drew attention. No candidate's wife had traveled with her husband on the campaign trail before. People also recognized her as the radio actress Evita Duarte. They had become the nation's ultimate power couple.

Argentine political candidates usually belonged to a specific political group. Perón, however, led a coalition, or group of political groups. He and Evita called their supporters the *descamisados*, which means "shirtless ones." This name drew attention to the fact that Perón's supporters worked for a living instead of dressing in fine suits and ties and leading privileged lives, like the oligarchy. Perón was frequently photographed wearing a simple button-up shirt with the sleeves rolled up to his elbows. This was a symbol of his willingness to work hard like the working class.

The goodwill of Perón's supporters was great, but the bitterness of his opponents was just as great. Critics said he was a fascist. They spread gossip and rumors about Evita. The campaign months between the Day of Revolution and election day in February were full of tension, arguments, and even violence. Would this man, who had been kicked out of the government and forced out of the country just a few months before, become the country's leader after all?

As it turned out, Juan Perón did win the election, with 52 percent of the vote. On June 4, 1946, after a formal banquet, he was inaugurated as president of Argentina. The next day, Juan and Evita Perón moved into the lavish, 283-room presidential palace, located in Palermo, Buenos Aires's finest suburb. Evita was now the first lady of Argentina.

Ironically, Evita's new neighbors were the oligarchy—the people who had looked down on her as an actress and had fought against her husband's election. Evita had risen from poverty to wealth and power, but she still lived in a neighborhood where the people wanted nothing to do with her.

CHAPTER SIX

First Lady

W HEN JUAN PERÓN BEGAN HIS TERM as president, he started building what he called the New Argentina. Whether anyone realized it yet or not, Evita was important to this plan for the country. She was a tireless supporter of Juan Perón's politics, which became known as Peronism. Evita also made her own path in the government. She created a work space and a mission for herself. It was in her first months as Argentina's first lady that Evita shaped the role that would earn her the love and respect of millions—and the ridicule and dislike of many others. She, too, helped to build the New Argentina.

NONTRADITIONAL WORK

If there was any expectation placed on the wife of Argentina's president, it probably was to be seen and not heard. The first lady did not have official duties within the government. She did not speak publicly, and she did not have her own causes to promote. In fact, one of the first lady's significant roles was to receive gifts. It was customary for people who visited the president or who asked favors of him to give gifts to the first lady. These gifts might be jewelry, fine china, or other luxuries.

Evita enjoyed receiving the gifts, but she refused to be just a

In August 1947, Eva Perón attended the Inter-American Conference for Peace and Security, held in Rio de Janeiro, Brazil.

traditional first lady. She believed that she had more important work to do. A few years later she wrote,

> **I was not only the wife of the President of the Republic, I was also the wife of the Leader of the Argentines. I had to have a double personality to correspond with Perón's double personality. One, Eva Perón, wife of the President, whose work is simple and agreeable, a holiday job of receiving honors, of gala performances; the other, "Evita," wife of the Leader of a people who have placed all their faith in him, all their hope and all their love. . . .**
>
> **I am . . . "Evita," a link stretched between the hopes of the people and the fulfilling hands of Perón,**
>
> **Argentina's first woman Peronista. . . .**

Beginning in her first weeks as first lady, Evita worked to be that link, or bridge, between the descamisados and President Perón. This, she believed, was her true mission in life.

Evita's first act was to visit factories and talk with workers and union leaders. At union meetings, her assistant took notes and made suggestions to the first lady. Evita may have felt shy in those first weeks, but she soon filled her new role eagerly. During passionate speeches, she used her hands to gesture emphatically and creased her brow with sincerity. Her actor's voice, rising and falling with emotion, snapped people to attention. From the beginning, she repeatedly told the working class that Juan Perón was devoted to them. She said,

> **" Perón is everything.**
> **He is the soul, the nerve, the hope and the reality of the Argentine people. "**

Next, Evita began to work a few days a week in a spare office in a government building. Soon, however, she moved her offices to the ministry of labor, where they would remain until her death. It was here that she found a perfect fit between her own strengths and a need of the Argentine people: the need for social aid for the poor and the working class. At first, Evita met with people who had union connections. They came to ask for help for a sick child or a poor mother. Evita listened, and within a few days she provided a solution—hospital treatment, housing, or whatever best fit the need. Evita knew what it was like to grow up on the outside, without privilege. Now that she was in the inner circle of power, she reached out to people who were excluded.

Evita also helped workers to form unions. She helped them figure out how to set up a legal union, and she made speeches in their support. When unions held elections, she made sure that Peronist members were able to show up to vote, even if that meant providing taxi rides for them. These trade unions helped workers obtain fair wages, benefits, more reasonable working hours, safer working conditions, and so on. Previous governments had never addressed these concerns.

GRATITUDE AND CRITICISM

Evita's devotion to working people earned both gratitude and criticism. People she helped saw her as something like a miracle worker. This was the first time they had seen a powerful person take active steps to help the poor. Evita was making visible progress toward creating the New Argentina.

On the other hand, some politicians and military leaders thought Evita was overstepping her boundaries. No first lady had ever set up offices for her own work. Evita was criticized, too, for putting her own family members in government positions that they were not qualified to hold. For instance, Evita's brother Juan Duarte received the appointment of private presidential secretary. His job was to decide who would be allowed to meet with President Perón. People grumbled that Evita would influence Juan's decisions. They saw this as yet another example of how Evita had too much influence over the president.

Argentine newspapers were generally not supportive of Perón. Evita tackled this problem in her typical fashion: she used her power to create a solution that pleased her. In this case, she bought the newspaper *Democracia* in early 1947. It was a small paper that published about six thousand copies per issue. Under Evita's ownership, the editors began filling the pages with pleasing photographs of Evita. They ran articles that supported Peronism. When Evita attended a festive event, they covered the evening in detail and published photographs of her dressed in beautiful gowns, furs, and jewels. The working class, especially housewives, loved this new approach. *Democracia*'s sales

Eva Perón reads a copy of the *Democracia*, the newspaper she bought in early 1947.

soared. An issue with lots of details and photographs from a festive gala would sell around 400,000 copies.

THE RAINBOW TOUR

In June 1947, Evita traveled overseas for the first time in her life. She had received an invitation from Spain's dictator, Francisco Franco, to visit his country. At this time, Spain's government was fascist, and Argentina was Spain's only friend. After World War II, Spain had fallen into hunger and poverty. Argentina loaned the country money to buy wheat. Juan Perón, however, chose not to visit Spain in person for fear that other world powers would conclude that he was a fascist. Evita, however, had more freedom and accepted the invitation to visit Spain.

Evita planned a major European tour around her trip to Spain. The purpose of this trip, according to the Argentine government, would be to unfurl a "rainbow of beauty" between the New World and the Old Word. Her trip came to be called the Rainbow Tour.

The night before Evita's journey, she was given a farewell reception. Evita said,

> **I am going as the representative of the working people, of my dear descamisados. I leave my heart behind with them.**

She did not say anything about loving or representing well-to-do Argentines. When she went to the airport the next day, a crowd of her supporters was there to bid her farewell. The trip was off to a festive start.

When Evita's airplane landed in Madrid, Spain, she exited the plane to an enthusiastic welcome. Three million people crowded into the capital city to see Evita. People ran alongside her car as it carried her through the streets. They treated her like a celebrity, and indeed, she was a celebrity to them. Few important people from other countries visited Spain at this time, for much the same reason that Juan Perón had chosen not to come. As a result, Evita's visit seemed that much more special and exciting. In addition, the people of Spain knew that Argentina had helped Spain with its food crisis. Many of them felt goodwill toward the first lady for this aid.

Evita's fifteen-day stay in Spain was filled with events and entertainment. She ate delicious meals at banquets in her honor. She was treated to plays, folk dance performances, and a bullfight that showcased Spain's culture. To top it all off, Franco awarded Evita the country's highest honor, the Grand Cross of Isabella the Catholic.

It was only when Evita was in her private room at night that she showed the strain of being away from home. She refused to sleep in her room alone, and she asked Liliane Guardo, her traveling companion, to sleep in the room with her.

News and details of Evita's Rainbow Tour were reported around the world. In the United States, *Time* magazine featured her face on the cover of the July 14, 1947, issue. In Europe, people were eager to see her for themselves.

Evita left Spain and continued her tour of Europe. In Italy, she was granted the rare honor of a private meeting with Pope Pius XII.

On July 2, 1947, during Eva Perón's goodwill tour of Europe, the first lady rode through the streets of Milan and was greeted by an adoring crowd.

Next, she visited Lisbon, the capital of Portugal. Then, in France, she received the Legion of Honor, the country's highest honor. Her last European stop was Switzerland. Evita had planned to visit England and to have tea with the queen in London. However, scheduling difficulties made it impossible for Evita to reach London before the queen left the city for her summer residence. Evita felt rejected, and she canceled her trip to England.

Evita returned home by ship, aboard the *Buenos Aires*. She stopped in Rio de Janeiro, Brazil, where she attended the Inter-American Conference for Peace and Security. She attended banquets and gave a press conference. Evita told the media,

> **" In my country all I do is aid the working class. "**

HOME AGAIN

When Evita finally arrived home, thousands of Argentines welcomed her at the docks. Evita was exhausted, but she stopped long enough to make a short speech, mentioning "my three loves: my country, my descamisados and my dear General Perón." The Rainbow Tour had lasted three months.

Not all Argentines were proud of Evita and her goodwill tour. There was grumbling about the trip's huge price tag. There were rumors that Evita had planned the whole trip just to get to Switzerland to deposit

LILIANE GUARDO

Evita was becoming one of the most famous faces in Argentina, but she allowed few people to be close to her—to see what she was like "behind the scenes." She made an exception for Liliane Guardo.

Liliane was the wife of the majority leader in Congress. When Evita met her, Liliane was a full-time mother raising four children. Evita persuaded Liliane to begin coming to her office at the ministry of labor. While Evita met with union members, Liliane would sit quietly. Evita once told Liliane, "It gives me so much peace to see you sitting there."

Evita could be demanding of Liliane's time. When Liliane wanted to go home to be with her children, Evita would ask her to stay. When Liliane's family went to the seaside for the summer, Evita made sure that Liliane spent weekdays in Buenos Aires with her.

Liliane did not give Evita political advice. Instead, Evita relied on Liliane for guidance in matters of style and culture. Liliane helped her sort through the gifts of china and jewelry that were given to the first lady. Liliane taught her how to recognize the quality pieces. Liliane helped Evita shop for jewelry and clothes, and she gave the first lady advice on how to dress tastefully for specific occasions. Later, when Evita traveled to Europe on a goodwill tour, she insisted that Liliane come along as her companion.

Evita did not share deep secrets with Liliane, but she did allow Liliane to see her weaknesses and vulnerabilities. In having this privilege, Liliane was unique.

money in a secret bank account. The government shut down two Argentine newspapers that printed unfavorable reports of the trip. Members of the oligarchy who frequently traveled to Europe accused Evita of trying to imitate them. They refused to accept her as an equal, regardless of her status as the president's wife and her residence in their own neighborhood. To these people, Evita would always be an outsider.

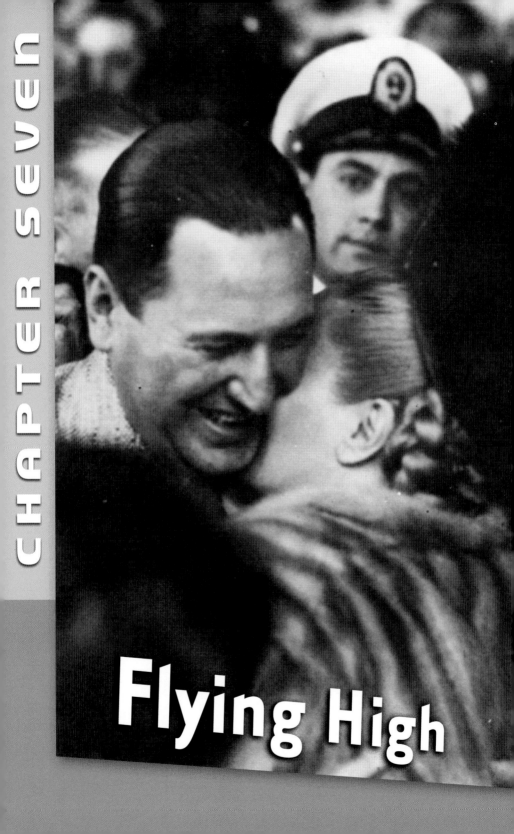

CHAPTER SEVEN

Flying High

IF THERE WAS ANYTHING THAT EVITA LOVED more than her descamisados, it was Juan Perón. She did not simply make him part of her life. She made him her entire life. His goals were her goals, and his battles were her battles. Her chosen work was designed to further Peronism and to strengthen Juan's leadership and power. Evita wrote,

> **I had decided to follow Perón, but I was not resigned to follow him from a distance, knowing that he was surrounded by enemies and ambitious men, who disguised themselves with friendly words—and by friends who didn't feel even the heat of the shadow of his ideals.**
>
> **I wanted to spend the days and the nights of his life with him, in the peace of his rests, and in the battles of his fight.**
>
> **I already knew that, like a condor, he was flying high and alone . . . and yet I had to fly with him!**

President Juan Perón greets Eva upon her return from her three-month tour of Europe in 1947.

And so it was that Juan and Evita Perón, each having risen from the lower class to fame and power, now ruled the country.

"Ruling" the country may be a strong way of stating it, but that is what Juan Perón did. Over the years of his first term in office, he became more and more like a dictator, a leader who has complete power over the entire country. But this happened gradually.

WOMEN'S SUFFRAGE

Evita may have been Juan Perón's biggest supporter, but she had been unable to vote for him in the election. At this point in time, only men could vote in Argentina. Since the early 1900s, there had been a growing woman's suffrage movement. Argentine women had watched as women in the United States gained the right to vote in 1920. Women in Britain over age thirty had won the right to vote in 1918, and then ten years later women were given the same voting rights as men. In 1944, women in France had gained the right to vote. But in Argentina, no women—not even the powerful women of the oligarchy—could vote. By the time Perón was president, though, the time for change seemed right.

Evita spoke publicly about the need for women's suffrage. Since Evita's political causes were Juan's causes, it was understood that the president was in favor of women's suffrage, too. When the matter came before Argentina's congress in 1947, a bill for women's suffrage was signed into law.

To Evita, this historic change meant that the number of potential voters for Perón had increased significantly. She told women, "To be a Peronist is, for a woman, to be loyal and to have blind confidence in Perón." She urged women to set up Peronist Women's Party offices

THE PERONIST WOMEN'S PARTY

Before women gained the right to vote, their participation in political parties was unlikely. After 1947, however, women represented a huge source of untapped political support. In 1949, Juan and Evita executed a plan to draw in these voters. They held a political rally in Luna Park stadium. About six thousand members of the Peronist party attended. President Perón gave an opening speech. Then Evita led the women to a separate area and delivered a speech of her own.

Evita spoke about loyalty to Perón, and she talked about the rights of working women. But the highlight of her speech was her proposal to create the Peronist Women's Party. Evita herself would head this party in her first official political appointment. The idea was groundbreaking. Women—not just the women at the rally, but women throughout the country—responded by the thousands. By 1952, the year of Evita's death, the Peronist Women's Party had half a million members.

throughout the country. Just as she had urged workers to unite in support of Perón, she encouraged women to do the same.

TRADITIONAL CHARITY

One of Evita's first priorities as first lady was to help the poor who went to her office at the ministry of labor. In the midst of world travels, fiery speeches, and securing women's suffrage, sitting down to talk with poor citizens was the least glamorous of Evita's endeavors. However, this work was closest to Evita's heart. Instead of letting it fade away quietly, as many busy politicians might have done, she pursued this work wholeheartedly.

Evita knew about a charitable organization whose mission was to help the poor and needy. The Beneficent Society was run by aging, wealthy women of the oligarchy. The society established orphanages and found housing for the elderly. It also operated some hospitals and a sanitarium, a special hospital for long-term care. The society did not always show warmth or respect to the people it helped. For example, the orphans had to shave their heads and wear blue uniforms. At Christmas, they had to go out on the streets and beg for donations to the society. Women who received aid often had to sew clothes for women of the oligarchy. Nurses in the society's hospitals were paid half the nation's minimum wage.

According to custom, the country's first lady served as honorary president of the Beneficent Society. As the story goes, the wealthy women of this society did not want Evita to be their honorary president. They sent word that she was too young to fill the role. Evita, stung by their rejection, shut down the Beneficent Society. She told the ladies that the New Argentina had no use for their kind of charity. Now, "social justice" would ensure that the needy were cared for.

What was Evita's idea of social justice in the New Argentina? For the time being, she turned her attention to the needy people who contacted her at the ministry of labor. By early 1948, she was receiving about 12,000 letters a day. These people wrote of hardship and poverty. They needed basics such as food, medicine, clothing, and shelter. People were given appointments to speak with Evita, who would decide what kind of help to give to each person. Out of this work grew the Eva Perón Foundation.

THE EVA PERÓN FOUNDATION

The need for Evita's help was much greater than what she could manage alone. She needed an organization to carry out her ideas on a larger scale. In July 1948, she established the Eva Perón Foundation. She did not want her organization to be like the Beneficent Society or other charities that she had seen in Europe—all organized by wealthy people. Evita observed that these charities were "created according to the criteria of the rich. . . . [W]hen the rich think about the poor they have poor ideas."

The Eva Perón Foundation received money from many different sources. Some funding came from the government, and some came from unions and businesses. Huge amounts of goods were donated, too. The foundation used the money to pay its employees and to buy clothing and other items that were given to people in need. Each year the foundation gave out thousands of pairs of shoes, sewing machines, cooking pots, and other necessities.

Large amounts of money flowed into the foundation. None of it was recorded or tracked in a bookkeeping system. Evita rejected the idea that she should provide an accounting of money received and money spent. She said, "Keeping books on charity is capitalistic nonsense. I just use the money for the poor. I can't stop to count it." Some people were suspicious that Evita used some of the money to buy luxuries for herself. She was regularly photographed wearing expensive jewels, furs, and designer gowns. But there was never any evidence to prove that she misused money in this way.

The foundation provided food, clothing, and shelter to the needy, but it went beyond these basic goals. It also provided scholarships to students and tools to workers. The foundation built schools, houses, and hospitals. Evita refused to call any of these actions charity. She preferred the term *social aid*. She wrote,

> **Charity humiliates, and social aid dignifies. . . .**
> **Charity prolongs the situation;**
> **social aid solves it. . . .**
> **Charity is the generosity of the fortunate;**
> **social aid remedies social inequalities.**

Even after the foundation was established, Evita continued her custom of meeting personally with people to discuss their needs. Each day, the waiting areas were crowded. Newspapers printed photographs of Evita meeting with citizens, hugging them, reaching a hand out to them, and examining documents with them at her desk. These photographs helped show the nation what the foundation was doing. The photographs and accompanying captions or articles were also wonderful publicity for President Perón and his government. Here was proof that this government cared about the ordinary

In 1949 Eva Perón founded the Children's City, a community designed for the care of children ages two to seven who were orphans or whose parents could not care for them.

citizen, the hardworking laborers, and the poor. Here was evidence of the New Argentina.

Over the next four years, the Eva Perón Foundation built a thousand schools and more than sixty hospitals. It set up training schools for nurses, who would then work in health-care clinics in city slums and rural towns. It built housing for single working women in Buenos Aires. It also provided housing for single mothers and the elderly. The foundation even built a special "children's city." Its small-scale buildings housed about two hundred orphans and children whose parents could not care for them. In 1951, the Health Care Train was sent on a tour of the country. Volunteers provided free medical and dental checkups and other health care services.

A "FANATIC"

Evita kept a grueling schedule. She woke up each morning at 5:30 AM, ate breakfast with Juan, and commuted to work at the ministry of labor. At 8:00 AM she began meeting with the crowds of people who awaited her. At midday, she and Juan took a *siesta*, or long lunch break. Then she was back at work, sometimes until midnight. On other evenings, she dressed in the gowns and jewels that so delighted her and attended parties and other events.

Evita pushed herself so hard that she did not get enough rest. Speaking of the people who waited to speak with her, she said,

"All these people, you see? I am nothing—my work is everything. Time is my greatest enemy."

She pursued her work and her support of Peronism so enthusiastically that her critics called her a fanatic, someone who takes a passion to the extreme while ignoring reason. They intended it as an insult, but Evita chose to take it as a compliment. She said,

> **Only fanatics—who are idealists and partisan—do not give up. . . . To serve the people, one has to be prepared for anything—including death. . . . That is why I am fanatic. I would give my life for Perón and for the people.**

Evita's words seem to predict the future, for in the end, she *did* give her life—just not in the way she might have expected. Her health had begun to fail her, but she ignored her body's signals that something was wrong. Evita was suffering from cancer.

CHAPTER EIGHT

LEAL INTERPRETE
DE LOS "DESCAMISADOS"

UNION U. MUNICIPALES

Adherida a la C. G. T.   Personería Gremial No. 9

Bridge of Love

B Y THE TIME JUAN PERÓN'S FIRST TERM in office was coming to an end, Evita's power within Argentina was undeniable. Her work with unions had made her a champion of the working class. Her work with the Eva Perón Foundation had made her a champion of the poor. Her work with the Peronist Women's Party had made her a champion of women. Her face and her name were everywhere. Bridges, bus stations, ships, and even constellations had been named after her. She did what she wanted, subject only to Juan Perón's higher authority.

Over the years, Evita's personal style had changed to reflect her new public image. In the beginning, she had dressed like a movie star—elaborate hairdos, flashy dresses, and wide, floppy hats. It would have been easy to view her, a former actress, as simply playing the role of the first lady. But gradually she had begun to dress with more taste and less flash. She now had a more functional hairdo: a sleek, braided bun. It became clear that she was not playing a part; she was living the part, and the part was her mission in life.

MISSION IN LIFE

Not long before the Rainbow Tour of Europe in 1947, Evita met a journalist named Manuel Penella da Silva. He persuaded Evita that her autobiography should be written. He would ghostwrite it himself, meaning that he would do the writing but they would

A poster of Eva Perón describes her as "Loyal Interpreter of the '*Descamisados*,'" (the "shirtless" working class).

put Evita's name on the cover as author. Work on the book began several years later, in 1950.

During the writing process, Evita and da Silva would meet and talk. Then da Silva would write chapters as though Evita herself had written them. Evita was acutely aware of the image that the book would project. At first, she aimed for an idealized version of herself. Later she changed her mind and presented a more down-to-earth, gritty Evita. She stressed her connection to the poor and her strong dislike of the rich.

A typical autobiography gives an account of the writer's birth and childhood, but Evita had never discussed these details about herself. Nor does the autobiography. She gives only brief, vague glimpses into her past and focuses on generalities of wealth and poverty. She does not state where she was born, but she observes, "There were many more poor than rich in the spot where I spent my childhood. . . ." She does not describe her daily life as a child, but she does say,

> Until I was eleven years old I believed that there were poor just as there was grass, and that there were rich just as there were trees. One day I heard for the first time, from the lips of a working-man, that there were poor because the rich were too rich; and that revelation made a strong impression on me.

The ghostwritten autobiography of Evita was passed to several key people for comment and approval. At first Juan Perón did not approve of the manuscript that da Silva had produced. Juan hired Raúl Mende, his speechwriter, to rework the manuscript. In the end, the book contained passages that sounded like speeches, as well as plenty of Peronist propaganda. Evita, however, accepted the book. In its prologue, she states,

> **... neither my life nor my heart belongs to me, and nothing of all that I am or have is mine. All that I am, all that I have, all that I think and all that I feel, belongs to Perón.**

The autobiography, titled *La Razón de Mi Vida* (*My Mission in Life*), was published in 1951, after Evita fell gravely ill with cancer. In 1950, however—the year that she and da Silva wrote the first draft— Evita was setting her sights on her next big goal in life. She was ready to be the country's vice president.

ELECTION YEAR

In 1951 there would be an election. Starting the moment Juan was elected to the presidency, Evita had never stopped giving pro-Perón speeches. Now, however, the coming election was a subject of increasing importance. There was no question that Juan Perón would run for reelection. But in this election, Evita had a new ambition. She wanted to run for vice president on the ticket with her husband.

Evita did not make a public announcement about running for

vice president. Instead, she let union leaders know that she wanted to run, and they promised her their support. It was the union leaders who organized the massive rally on August 22, 1951, on the *Avenida 9 de Julio*. It was they who hung the billboard-size portraits of Juan and Eva Perón with the "bridge of love," or banner, between them. It was the CGT president who announced to the crowd, "We shall wait here for her decision. We shall not move until she gives us a reply in accordance with the desires of the people."

Evita Perón had overcome many obstacles to reach this point in her life and career. The evening was one of triumph for her. Even though she refused to say clearly that she would accept the nomination, and even though she afterward declined the nomination, she had reached a mountain peak. She had climbed up from the tiny house by the railroad tracks in Los Toldos to stand next to the most powerful man in Argentina. Indeed, some said that it was Evita who truly held the power, as shown by the crowd's greater interest in Evita's decision than in Juan's acceptance speech.

Soon after that night, however, Evita was forced to realize the seriousness of her health problems. She became rapidly weaker, but she still resisted treatment. Finally she was hospitalized, and she reluctantly agreed to let doctors operate.

On election day in November, Evita was too weak to leave her hospital bed. This was the first election in which Argentine women had the right to vote, however, and Evita did not pass up the historic opportunity. A special ballot box was brought to her hospital bed, and she was photographed placing her ballot in it.

Throughout Argentina, 4 million women turned out to vote. Not all of them voted for Perón or Peronist candidates, but a majority of them did. They helped put Perón in office for a second term as

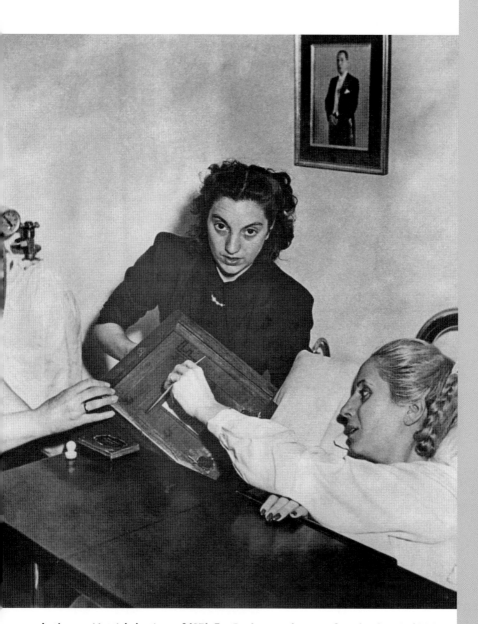

In the presidential elections of 1951, Eva Perón casts her vote from her hospital bed.

POLITICAL PARTIES

The party that opposed the Peronists in the election of 1951 was the Radical Civic Union (RCU). The party's supporters are called radicals. Founded in 1891, the Radical Civic Union is the oldest political party in Argentina. Traditionally, the radicals have valued individuals' rights and open, fair elections. They have won support from the middle class. During Evita's lifetime, the radicals opposed the conservatives (favored by the oligarchy) and then the Peronists (favored by the working class).

Today, the RCU is one of the two main political parties in Argentina. The other chief party is the Justicialist Party. In the early 1970s Juan Perón founded this party to reunite Peronists. Cristina Kirchner, who became president of Argentina in 2007, is a member of the Justicialist Party.

Cristina Fernández de Kirchner holds a staff and gestures during her inauguration as President of Argentina, December 10, 2007.

president. In addition, many women ran for office. In that election, twenty-nine women were elected to Argentina's congress, and other women were elected to offices in provinces and towns throughout the country. It was a momentous election day in Argentina's history, and Evita Perón had helped lead the nation to this point.

FINAL APPEARANCE AND DEATH

Evita's last public appearance was at Juan's side on the day of his inauguration to his second term in office. On June 4, 1952, she rode with him through the streets in an open-air car and waved at supporters. The change in Evita's appearance was extreme. Her body was frail and pale. A huge fur coat disguised the fact that she weighed only 80 pounds. Although it appeared that she was standing beside Perón, a brace hidden in the fur coat was holding her up. She was too weak to stand unaided, and she was in terrible pain.

By now, there had been a public announcement of Evita's illness. The announcement stated that she had "an anemia of great intensity." In truth, Evita had cancer of the uterus, but only a select few people knew the exact diagnosis. Not even Evita was told that she had cancer. She did, however, understand how seriously ill she was. She wrote a will in which she asserted her devotion to Juan Perón and her beloved descamisados:

I want to live with Perón and with my People forever. That is my absolute and final wish, and it will therefore also be, when my time is up, the last wish of my heart. Wherever Perón is, and wherever my descamisados are, there, too, will be my heart to love them with all the strength of my life and with all the fanaticism of my soul.

June 12, 1952. Following Juan Perón's second inauguration as president, he and Eva wave to supporters as they ride down the Avenida de Mayo in Buenos Aires.

Evita's desire to remain with those she loved came true, in a way. Even after her death, she remained alive in spirit with the descamisados of Argentina.

Besides writing her will, Evita uttered many "last words." In her final months and weeks, she grew increasingly harsh with her enemies, increasingly fearful of plots against Juan, and increasingly passionate about protecting the poor. "If it is necessary," she said, "we will execute justice with our own hands." A few years later, some political groups would use these threatening words to encourage and defend violent political acts.

Evita lived only a few weeks past Juan's inauguration. She died on July 26, 1952. She was thirty-three years old. An announcement of her death was broadcast on the radio, and the city of Buenos Aires immediately shut down in mourning.

FATHER HERNÁN BENÍTEZ

One of the few people Evita trusted was Father Hernán Benítez, a Catholic priest. Just as Liliane Guardo gave Evita advice on style and culture, Benítez gave Evita advice on social and moral problems. She took Benítez on the Rainbow Tour with her.

When Evita was first lady, Benítez was graduate dean (head of students who already had one degree) of the National University of Buenos Aires. He was also a professor of philosophy. Today he is the spiritual director of the Eva Perón Foundation. In remembering Evita's death, he told an interviewer,

> The most despised woman in Argentina had died. She was also, without doubt, the most loved person in our history. She left behind tremendous mistakes, but also tremendous successes.

With his words, Benítez summed up the paradox of Evita: she was a woman who achieved both failure and success, and a woman who was both despised and loved.

CHAPTER NINE

The Legend

WHEN EVITA DIED, MILLIONS OF ARGENTINES plunged into sorrow and mourning. People showed their grief in different ways, from the president in the capital to the campesinos in the pampa. The government shut down for two days, and flags were flown at half-mast for ten days. Union leaders told members to take two days off from work and to wear a black tie and jacket for a month to signify mourning. In the neighborhoods, thousands of people made small altars of Evita's photograph surrounded by flowers. There were mass demonstrations of grief as the days went on.

PUBLIC VIEWING

Juan Perón did not want to bury his wife's body. Instead, he wanted it preserved so that people could "visit" Evita and pay respect to her for years to come. He asked an expert to begin the process of preserving her body so that it would look as if she were alive, but sleeping. Meanwhile, Juan planned for a public viewing and funeral for Evita.

When Evita's death was announced, it was also announced that her body would be brought to the ministry of labor the next day. Here, mourners could view the body. Like a rising tide, masses of people began to gather outside the building where Evita had worked. They brought flowers and stacked them in ever-growing piles. Ignoring the cold, rainy winter weather, they waited. For ten blocks in all directions, mourners clogged the

In August 1952, crowds thronged the ministry of labor, waiting for a turn to walk by Eva Perón's coffin.

streets. The next day, when Evita's body was brought to the building, eight people were crushed to death as the crowd pressed forward to see the first lady.

At last, mourners filed past Evita's casket inside the ministry of labor. Some people brushed their fingers across the casket, while others bent and kissed the glass cover. Some people crossed themselves,

Eva Perón's body, in its glass-covered coffin, was on display for sixteen days so that countless mourners could pay their respects.

EVA PERÓN

and others sobbed. A three-day public viewing had been planned, but so many people wanted to see the first lady that the viewing was extended. People lined up in the wintry weather for thirteen more days for a chance to file past the casket. Finally, the body was taken to the congress building for an official delivery of honors. From there, it was taken to a room in the CGT headquarters. Here, the work of preserving Evita's body would continue for the next three years.

MISSING CORPSE

At the time of Evita's death, Argentina's economy was having serious problems. Exports of wheat and beef had once helped to make the nation prosperous. Since 1945, production of wheat and beef had declined significantly. To make matters worse, a drought in the pampa had reduced production even further. The country was losing export business, which meant it was losing income. Within Argentina, the sale of beef was rationed to make sure the supply did not run out. Rising prices gobbled up the higher wages Perón had once won for the workers, and they struggled to pay for necessities.

Once a wealthy nation, Argentina was now in financial trouble. Many people blamed Juan Perón and Peronism. While the president still had loyal supporters, his opponents grew in number and in power. In 1955, in a coup d'etat, the military took control of the government. Perón fled the country and went into exile. During all this turmoil, Evita's body disappeared.

For years, no one seemed to know what had happened to Eva Perón's body. In truth, the military government had taken and hidden the body for political reasons. They hoped that the memory of Evita would fade. Without a body to visit and to remind people of her revolutionary message, perhaps Peronists would not try to overthrow this government.

People did not forget about Evita, however. Those who had loved and admired her told stories about how wonderful she had been. They called her Lady of Hope and Good Fairy because of her work for the poor. Many of the stories were inspired by reality but were not actually true.

In contrast, critics of Evita spoke out against her and told rumors about the first lady's greed for money and power. They accused her of using money from the Eva Perón Foundation to buy some of the expensive gowns, furs, and jewelry that she loved to wear. Both the White Myth and the Black Myth grew.

RETURN OF JUAN PERÓN

Juan Perón still had supporters within Argentina, and they used Evita's memory to strengthen their cause. They declared that, if Evita were alive, she would be one of them. In 1970 a group of Peronists kidnapped former Argentine president Aramburu, who had instructed the military to hide Evita's body. They tried to force him to tell them the location of the body, but he refused. They killed him and announced to newspapers that they would not release his body until Evita's body had been "returned to the people."

The secret of the body's location was now in the hands of someone no one suspected. The military officers who had hidden Evita's body had written down the location in a letter. They delivered the letter, sealed in an envelope, to then-president Aramburu. Without reading the letter, Aramburu had placed it in the keeping of his lawyer. His instructions were to deliver the letter four weeks after his death to whoever was president of Argentina.

Later, after police finally discovered Aramburu's body, the letter was delivered to President Lanusse. He arranged for the body to be removed from its hiding place in a cemetery in Milan, Italy. The body was then delivered to Juan Perón, who was still in exile in Spain. The location of the body was not announced publicly. To nearly everyone, the location of the body would remain a mystery until 1974, when it was finally returned to Argentina.

In the early 1970s, changes took place within Argentina's government. Lanusse took office in March 1971. President Lanusse worked for a return to constitutional government, and he supported political freedom. He announced a return to party politics and free elections. This meant that voters, not the military, would determine who governed the country. Although Lanusse personally opposed Peronism, he allowed Peronists the freedoms that all political groups had.

With Lanusse in power, Juan Perón saw his chance to return to his homeland. He negotiated with Lanusse for his safe return. Lanusse agreed to drop several charges against the former president, including the charge of treason. Finally, after seventeen years in exile, Perón made a triumphant return to Argentina in November 1972. Perón brought with him the woman he had married, Isabel Martínez de Perón. Isabel showed great respect to the memory of Eva Perón. She mentioned Evita in interviews and said that she hoped to be like her.

Peronists had not given up the idea of Perón's returning to the presidency. When elections were scheduled for September 1973, Perón emerged as the presidential candidate to beat. Perón persuaded his supporters to put his wife, Isabel, on the ticket as his vice presidential running mate. The Perón-Perón ticket won by a large margin, and Juan Perón was back in power after seventeen years in exile. The victory, at least for Juan, was short-lived. He died on July 1, 1974, less than a year after taking office. Isabel Perón was now Argentina's president, but less than a year later, a new military coup overthrew the government.

FINAL RESTING PLACE

In November 1974, under Isabel Perón's government, Evita's body was finally returned to Argentina. The government had plans to build a giant memorial, inside of which the bodies of Argentine leaders would be buried. With the overthrow of Perón's government, this idea was abandoned.

In the end, Evita's body was turned over to her sisters, who buried her in La Recoleta Cemetery in Buenos Aires. Evita's mother, who died in 1971, was already buried there. The Duarte family tomb is small and nondescript. Evita's casket was placed in a locked space deep underneath the tomb. This specially constructed space is inaccessible to grave robbers and can withstand bombs.

Ironically, Evita's final resting place is not among the poor or the working class. La Recoleta Cemetery is the premier cemetery of the oligarchy, the people whom Evita had always opposed.

THE LEGEND LIVES ON

More than half a century has passed since Eva Perón died, but the legend of her life and death has remained vibrantly alive.

In 1978, two years after the burial in La Recoleta Cemetery, a

An American movie poster advertises *Evita*, a 1996 film starring
Madonna and Antonio Banderas.

musical called *Evita* gained worldwide popularity. One of its signature songs is "Don't Cry for Me Argentina." In 1996 *Evita* was made into a movie starring Madonna, Jonathan Pryce, and Antonio Banderas. The movie won three Golden Globe Awards and an Oscar. Over the years, filmmakers have made a number of documentaries of Eva Perón's life.

On Internet auction sites, collectors buy and sell Evita-themed memorabilia. Items include photographs, autographs, stamps, coins, newspaper articles, magazine covers, special publications, and more.

In 1998, the family of Eva Perón founded the Eva Perón Historical Research Foundation and set up an official Eva Perón website. In 2002, on the fiftieth anniversary of Evita's death, the Evita Museum was established in Buenos Aires. It displays informative exhibits; clothing, shoes, and hats worn by Evita; and a funeral mask (a plaster cast, or copy, made of Evita's face after her death).

A LEGACY OF ACTION

Upon Evita's death, Juan Perón promised to fulfill her duties at the ministry of labor. For a short time, he went to her office and received the poor and destitute. He listened to their stories and arranged aid for them. While Evita had found this work to be fulfilling, Juan found it to be unbearably dull. He soon turned the work over to others.

Those who took over the leadership of the Eva Perón Foundation helped Evita's legacy of social action live on. At the end of Evita's life, the care of those in need remained uppermost in her concerns. In *Mi Mensaje*, Evita expresses deep anger and disappointment with people who *should* care for the poor but do not:

> **" I reproach them for having abandoned the poor, the humble, the descamisados, the sick . . . and for having preferred, instead, the glory and the honors of the oligarchy. "**

Anyone wishing to follow in Evita's footsteps can rely on Evita's method of getting started. She was asked how she started the work that became the Eva Perón Foundation. Her answer was simple:

> **" And we began. Bit by bit. I couldn't say exactly on what day. What I do know is that at first I attended to everything myself. Then I had to ask for help. "**

Thus, a part of Evita's legacy is an example of social action—the example to begin, little by little, where one is, and to work from there. Those who practice social aid are performing the work that was closest to Evita's heart.

MY MESSAGE

In 1987 a historian published *Mi Mensaje (My Message)*, the deathbed message of Eva Perón. It had lain undiscovered for years in a government archive. Scholars argue about whether Evita wrote any or all of the manuscript. It is likely that, like *My Mission in Life*, it was dictated in part by Evita and was ghost-written and edited by someone else.

In *Mi Mensaje* Evita asserts, once again, her love for the descamisados. She expresses concern about who will take care of them after she is gone:

> Recently, in the hours of my illness, I have thought
> often of this message from my heart. . . .
> I love the descamisados, the women, the workers
> of my people too much, and, by extension,
> I love all the world's exploited people . . .
> too much to keep quiet. . . .
> *My Message* is for them: for my people and for all
> of humanity's people. . . .
> I want to incite the people. I want to ignite them
> with the fire of my heart.

Evita's final message to the world stresses a desire that others will take up her cause where she left off.

TIMELINE

1919	Born May 7
1935	Moves to Buenos Aires
1939	Forms a radio company with Pascual Pelliciotta
1943	Achieves success as a radio actress
1944	Meets Colonel Juan Domingo Perón
1945	Witnesses Revolution Day, October 17 Marries Juan Perón
1946	Becomes the first lady of Argentina Sets up office at ministry of labor

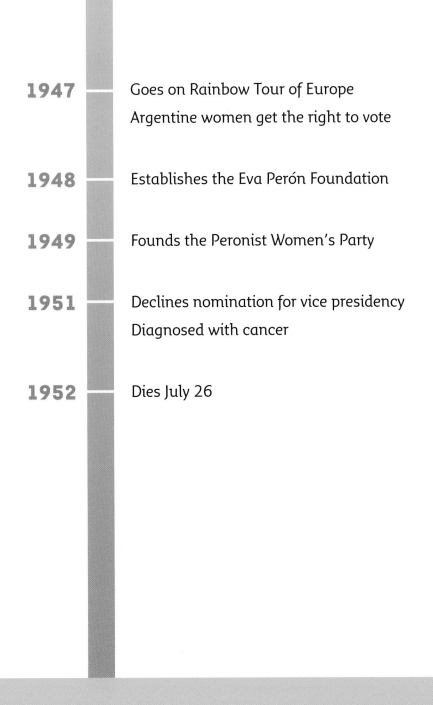

1947 — Goes on Rainbow Tour of Europe
Argentine women get the right to vote

1948 — Establishes the Eva Perón Foundation

1949 — Founds the Peronist Women's Party

1951 — Declines nomination for vice presidency
Diagnosed with cancer

1952 — Dies July 26

SOURCE NOTES

Boxed quotes unless otherwise noted

CHAPTER 1

p. 8, Nicholas Fraser and Marysa Navarro, *Evita: The Real Life of Eva Perón* (New York: W. W. Norton, 1996), p. 144.

p. 9, Fraser and Navarro, op. cit., p. 145.

p. 9-10, Fraser and Navarro, op. cit., p. 145.

p. 10, Fraser and Navarro, op. cit., p. 145.

p. 12, par. 2, Fraser and Navarro, op. cit., p. 146.

p. 12, par. 3, Fraser and Navarro, op. cit., p. 146.

p. 13, par. 1, Alicia Dujovne Ortiz, *Eva Perón*, 1995, trans. Shawn Fields (New York: St. Martin's Press, 1996), p. 267.

p. 13, Fraser and Navarro, op. cit., p. 146.

CHAPTER 2

p. 19, par. 1, Blanca Duarte, "Our True Life," www.evitaperon.org, par. 3, (accessed August 27, 2008).

p. 21, par. 3, Nicholas Fraser and Marysa Navarro, *Evita: The Real Life of Eva Perón* (New York: W. W. Norton, 1996), p. 8.

p. 23, par. 1, Duarte, op. cit., par. 14.

p. 25, par. 1, Fraser and Navarro, op. cit., p. 11.

p. 25, par. 2, Duarte, op. cit., par. 18.

CHAPTER 3

p. 30, par. 1, Nicholas Fraser and Marysa Navarro, *Evita: The Real Life of Eva Perón* (New York: W. W. Norton, 1996), p. 20.

p. 32, Fraser and Navarro, op. cit., p. 22.

p. 35, Evita Perón Historical Research Foundation, "To Be Evita," Part 1, trans. Dolane Larson, www.evitaperon.org, (accessed August 27, 2008).

CHAPTER 4

p. 37, par. 1, Eva Perón, *La Razón de Mi Vida*, 1953, reprinted as *Evita by Evita: Evita Duarte Perón Tells Her Own Story* (New York: Proteus, 1978), p. 17.

p. 40, par. 2, Nicholas Fraser and Marysa Navarro, *Evita: The Real Life of Eva Perón* (New York: W. W. Norton, 1996), p. 33.

p. 41, par. 2, Fraser and Navarro, op. cit., p. 41.

CHAPTER 5

p. 30, Eva Perón, *La Razón de Mi Vida,* 1953, reprinted as *Evita by Evita: Evita Duarte Perón Tells Her Own Story* (New York: Proteus, 1978), pp. 25, 26.

p. 30, par. 4, Nicholas Fraser and Marysa Navarro, *Evita: The Real Life of Eva Perón* (New York: W. W. Norton, 1996), p. 60.

p. 30, par. 4, Fraser and Navarro, op. cit., p. 61.

p. 31, par. 5, Fraser and Navarro, op. cit., p. 67.

CHAPTER 6

p. 60, Eva Perón, *La Razón de Mi Vida*, 1953, reprinted as *Evita by Evita: Evita Duarte Perón Tells Her Own Story* (New York: Proteus, 1978), pp. 58–59.

p. 61, Darlene R. Stille, *Eva Perón: First Lady of Argentina* (Minneapolis: Compass Point Books, 2006), pp. 57–58.

p. 64, Nicholas Fraser and Marysa Navarro, *Evita: The Real Life of Eva Perón* (New York: W. W. Norton, 1996), p. 90.

p. 67, Fraser and Navarro, op. cit., p. 99.

p. 67, par. 3, Fraser and Navarro, op. cit., p. 99.

p. 68, par. 2, Fraser and Navarro, op. cit., p. 80.

CHAPTER 7

p. 71, Eva Perón, *Mi Mensaje*, 1987, reprinted as *In My Own Words: Evita*, trans. Laura Dail (New York: New Press, 1996), p. 52.

p. 72, par. 5, Darlene R. Stille, *Eva Perón: First Lady of Argentina* (Minneapolis: Compass Point Books, 2006), p. 71.

p. 75, par. 2, Stille, op. cit., p. 76.

p. 75, par. 4, John Barnes, *Evita, First Lady: A Biography of Eva Perón* (New York: Grove Press, 1978), p. 115.

p. 76, Barnes, op. cit., p. 120.

p. 78, par. 4, Stille, op. cit., p. 82.

p. 79, Eva Perón, *Mi Mensaje*, 1987, reprinted as *In My Own Words: Evita*, trans. Laura Dail (New York: New Press, 1996), p. 57.

CHAPTER 8

p. 82, par. 3, Eva Perón, *La Razón* de Mi Vida, 1953, reprinted as *Evita by Evita: Evita Duarte Perón Tells Her Own Story* (New York: Proteus, 1978), p. 12.

p. 82, Perón, *La Razón*, op. cit., p. 7.

p. 83, Perón, *La Razón*, op. cit., Prologue (n.p.).

p. 84, par. 1, Nicholas Fraser and Marysa Navarro, *Evita: The Real Life of Eva Perón* (New York: W. W. Norton, 1996), p. 146.

p. 87, par. 3, Fraser and Navarro, op. cit., p. 149.

p. 87, Eva Perón, *Mi Mensaje*, 1987, reprinted as *In My Own Words: Evita*, trans. Laura Dail (New York: New Press, 1996), p. 87.

p. 88, par. 2, Fraser and Navarro, op. cit., p. 155.

p. 89, par. 3, Hernán Benítez, comments made in interview, *El Misterio Eva Peron*, DVD.

CHAPTER 9

p. 94, par. 4, Nicholas Fraser and Marysa Navarro, *Evita: The Real Life of Eva Perón* (New York: W. W. Norton, 1996), p. 186.

p. 99, Eva Perón. *Mi Mensaje*, 1987, reprinted as *In My Own Words: Evita*, trans. Laura Dail (New York: New Press, 1996), p. 75.

p. 99, "From 'Las Delicias' to the Fundación Eva Perón." (*Mundo Peronista*, 1 July 1954. Reprinted at www.evitaperon.org, Dolane Larson, trans. Accessed October 8, 2008), par. 14.

p. 101, par. 3, Perón, *Mi Mensaje*, op. cit., pp. 49, 50.

FURTHER INFORMATION

BOOKS

Blashfield, Jean F. *Argentina*. New York: Children's Press, 2007.

Spengler, Kremena. *Eva Perón: First Lady of the People*. Mankato, MN: Capstone Press, 2007.

Stille, Darlene R. *Eva Perón: First Lady of Argentina*. Minneapolis, MN: Compass Point Books, 2006.

WEBSITES

Evita Perón Historical Research Foundation

*This website was created by the family of Eva Perón. It contains biographical information and photographs.

www.evitaperon.org

Evita Museum

Get previews and descriptions of some of the exhibits at the Evita Museum in Buenos Aires.

www.welcomeargentina.com/ciudadbuenosaires/
eva-peron-museum.html

BIBLIOGRAPHY

Barnes, John. *Evita, First Lady: A Biography of Eva Perón.* New York: Grove Press, 1978.

Duarte, Blanca. "Our True Life." www.evitaperon.org (accessed August 27, 2008).

Evita Perón Historical Research Foundation. *To Be Evita.* Translated by Dolane Larson. www.evitaperon.org, (accessed August 27, 2008).

"From 'Las Delicias' to the Fundación Eva Perón." *Mundo Peronista,* July 1, 1954. Reprinted at www.evitaperon.org. Translated by Dolane Larson (accessed October 8, 2008).

Evita: The Woman Behind the Myth. Biography. VHS. 1996.

Fraser, Nicholas, and Marysa Navarro. *Evita: The Real Life of Eva Perón.* New York: W. W. Norton, 1996.

El Misterio Eva Peron. DVD. First Run Features, 1987.

Ortiz, Alicia Dujovne. *Eva Perón.* 1995. Translated by Shawn Fields. New York: St. Martin's Press, 1996.

———. *Mi Mensaje.* 1987. Reprinted as *In My Own Words: Evita.* Translated by Laura Dail. New York: New Press, 1996.

Perón, Eva. *La Razon de Mi Vida.* 1953. Reprinted as *Evita by Evita: Eva Duarte Perón Tells Her Own Story.* New York: Proteus Publishing Group, 1978.

Taylor, J. M. *Eva Perón: The Myths of a Woman.* Chicago University of Chicago Press, 1979.

INDEX

ABOUT THE AUTHOR

LESLI J. FAVOR is the author of more than twenty books for young adult readers and students. She holds a PhD in English from the University of North Texas. After graduating, she was assistant professor of English at Sul Ross State University Rio Grande College, in southwest Texas. She left that position to write full-time. Favor lives near Seattle with her husband, young son, two dogs, and horse.